Big Island Revealed

The Practical Big Island Travel Guide, For Planning Your Trip, Where to Stay, Activities to Do, What to Pack etc.

Collins Jake

Table of Contents

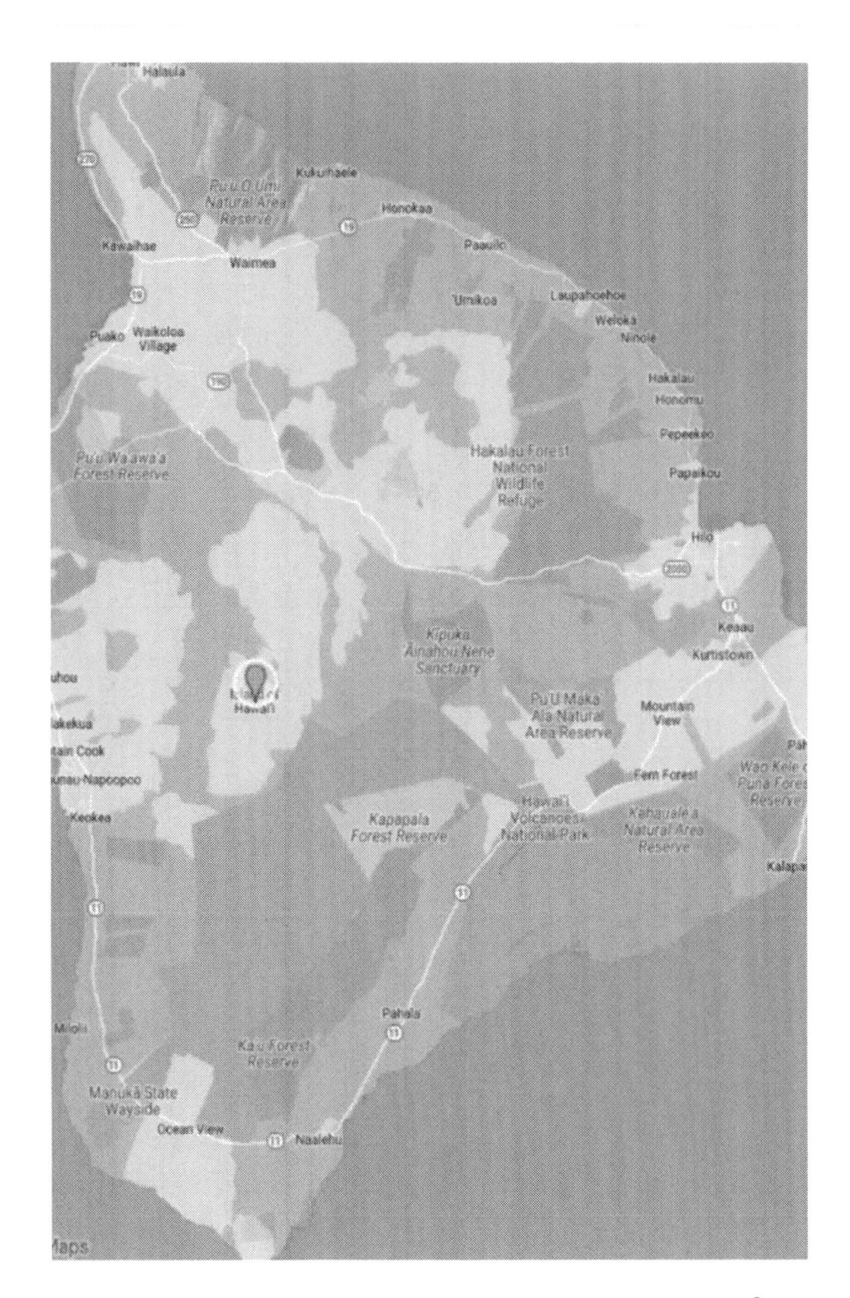
Halaula
Kukuihaele
Puu O Umi Natural Area Reserve
Honokaa
Kawaihae
Waimea
Paauilo
Umikoa
Laupahoehoe
Puako
Waikoloa Village
Ninole
Hakalau
Honomu
Pepeekeo
Pu'u Wa'awa'a Forest Reserve
Hakalau Forest National Wildlife Refuge
Papaikou
Hilo
Keaau
Kurtistown
Kipuka Ainahou Nene Sanctuary
Hawai'i
Pu'u Maka'Ala Natural Area Reserve
Mountain View
Fern Forest
Keokea
Kapapala Forest Reserve
Hawai'i Volcanoes National Park
Kahauale'a Natural Area Reserve
Pahala
Ka'u Forest Reserve
Manukā State Wayside
Ocean View
Naalehu

CHAPTER 1

Big Island Brief History

The Big Island, also known as Hawai'i Island, is one of the islands in the state of Hawai'i and the United States. It is located in the Pacific Ocean and is part of the Hawaiian archipelago. The island has a rich culture and history dating back to ancient times civilization.

The first known settlers of the Big Island were Polynesians who arrived around 1000 AD. They established a complex society and developed a unique culture that included a system of governance, agriculture, and trade. The island was ruled by a series of chiefs or ali'i, and the people followed a strict set of social and religious customs.

The first European to visit the Big Island was British explorer James Cook, who arrived in 1778. He named the island "Sandwich Islands" after the Fourth Earl of Sandwich, who sponsored his voyage. The island was later renamed Hawai'i after one of the chiefs who welcomed Cook.

In the 19th century, the Hawaiian Islands were united under the rule of King Kamehameha I, who established a monarchy on the islands. The Big Island became an important center of trade and commerce, and it played a significant role in the development of the Hawaiian Kingdom.

Today, the Big Island is a popular tourist destination known for its stunning natural beauty, including its beaches, waterfalls, and volcanic landscapes. The island is also home to a number of historical and cultural attractions, including the Hōnaunau National Historical Park, the Hawai'i Volcanoes National Park, and the Hulihe'e Palace.

CHAPTER 2

Activities in Big island

The Big Island of Hawaii is a popular vacation destination and offers a wide range of activities and attractions to enjoy throughout the year. Some popular activities to consider include:

Beaches

The Big Island is home to a number of beautiful beaches, including Hapuna Beach and Kauna'oa

Bay, which are great for swimming, sunbathing, and other beach activities.

Hiking

The Big Island offers a variety of hiking trails, ranging from easy nature walks to challenging backcountry trails. Popular hikes include the Waipi'o Valley Trail and the Kilauea Iki Trail.

Water sports

The Big Island is a great place for water sports such as snorkeling, scuba diving, and surfing. The Kealakekua Bay State Historical Park is a popular spot for snorkeling, and the island's rugged coastline offers some excellent surf breaks.

Golfing

The Big Island is home to a number of golf courses, including the Mauna Kea Golf Course and the Hualalai Golf Course, both of which offer stunning ocean views.

Cultural activities

The Big Island has a rich cultural history and offers a variety of activities to help visitors learn more about its history and traditions. These may include visiting cultural centers, attending hula performances, or participating in traditional Hawaiian activities such as lei-making (flower weaving) or ukulele (Hawaii guitar) lessons.

Shopping and Dining

The Big Island is home to a number of shopping and dining options, ranging from local farmer's markets to upscale restaurants. Popular shopping areas include the Hilo Farmers Market and the Kailua-Kona Village Market.

Volcano viewing

The Big Island is home to the active Kilauea volcano, which offers a variety of opportunities for viewing and learning about volcanic activity. Visitors can take guided tours of the volcano, attend ranger-led talks, or explore the volcano on their own.

No matter what time of year you visit the Big Island, there are plenty of activities and attractions to enjoy.

CHAPTER 3

Activities To Do By Month

There are many activities to do on the Big Island of Hawaii throughout the year, depending on your interests and the weather conditions. Here is a list of some popular activities and events to consider for each month:

January

-Hike to see the sunrise at Mauna Kea
-Visit the Hawaii Volcanoes National Park
-Take a whale-watching tour
-Go snorkeling or diving at Kealakekua Bay

February

-Attend the annual Waimea Cherry Blossom Heritage Festival
-Go skiing or snowboarding on Mauna Kea
-Take a ziplining tour through the rainforest
-Go horseback riding through the ranchlands

March

-Visit the Honaunau National Historical Park
-Take a coffee tour of the Kona region
-Go fishing off the coast of the Big Island
-Attend the Merrie Monarch Festival, a week-long celebration of hula and Hawaiian culture

April

-Take a boat tour to see the dolphins and whales
-Go surfing at one of the island's many beaches
-Visit the Hawaii Tropical Botanical Garden
-Attend the annual Paniolo Parade and Rodeo in Waimea

May

-Hike to see the Akaka Falls
-Go snorkeling or diving at Pohoiki Beach
-Take a boat tour to see the dolphins and whales
-Attend the annual Merrie Monarch Hula Festival

June

-Visit the Pu'ukohola Heiau National Historic Site
-Go surfing at one of the island's many beaches

-Take a boat tour to see the dolphins and whales
-Attend the annual Ironman World Championship triathlon

July

-Take a boat tour to see the dolphins and whales
-Go snorkeling or diving at Kealakekua Bay
-Visit the Hawaii Volcanoes National Park
-Attend the annual Paniolo Parade and Rodeo in Waimea

August

-Take a boat tour to see the dolphins and whales
-Go surfing at one of the island's many beaches
-Visit the Hawaii Tropical Botanical Garden
-Attend the annual Merrie Monarch Hula Festival

September

-Take a boat tour to see the dolphins and whales
-Go snorkeling or diving at Pohoiki Beach
-Visit the Honaunau National Historical Park
-Attend the annual Ironman World Championship triathlon

October

Hike to see the Akaka Falls
Go surfing at one of the island's many beaches
Take a boat tour to see the dolphins and whales
Attend the annual Merrie Monarch Hula Festival

November

-Take a boat tour to see the dolphins and whales
-Go snorkeling or diving at Kealakekua Bay
-Visit the Hawaii Volcanoes National Park
-Attend the annual Paniolo Parade and Rodeo in Waimea

December

-Take a boat tour to see the dolphins and whales
-Go surfing at one of the island's many beaches
-Visit the Hawaii Tropical Botanical Garden
-Attend the annual Merrie Monarch Hula Festival

This is just a small sample of the many activities and events available on the Big Island throughout the year. There are many other options to choose from as mentioned earlier in the Activities Chapter.

CHAPTER 4

Top 10 Attractions in Big Island

The Big Island of Hawaii, also known as the Island of Hawaii, is the largest and youngest island in the Hawaiian archipelago. It is home to a diverse range of attractions, including natural wonders, cultural and historical sites, and recreational activities. Here are some top attractions to consider when visiting the Big Island:

Mauna Kea Observatories

Mauna Kea Observatories are a group of telescopes and observatories located on the summit of Mauna Kea, a mountain on the island of Hawaii. The observatories are used for a variety of purposes, including studying the stars, planets, and other celestial objects. The summit of Mauna Kea is home to some of the world's most advanced telescopes, and the observatories are used by astronomers and researchers from around the world.

Tourists are welcome to visit the Mauna Kea Observatories, but it is important to note that the summit of Mauna Kea is at an altitude of 4,200 meters (13,800 feet) above sea level, and the thin air and cold temperatures can be challenging for some people. It is recommended that visitors acclimate to the altitude before visiting the observatories, and that they dress appropriately for the cold temperatures.

The Mauna Kea Visitor Information Station, located at the base of the mountain, offers educational programs about the observatories and the cultural and natural history of Mauna Kea. From the visitor station, visitors can take a guided tour of the observatories or visit the exhibits on their own. The tours and exhibits provide an opportunity to learn about the science being done at the observatories and to see the telescopes up close.

Overall, a visit to the Mauna Kea Observatories can be a unique and educational experience for tourists interested in astronomy and the natural beauty of Hawaii.

Kilauea

Kilauea is a volcano located on the island of Hawaii, also known as the Big Island. It is one of the most active volcanoes in the world and has been erupting continuously since 1983. Kilauea is a popular tourist destination and attracts visitors from all over the world.

There are several ways to experience Kilauea as a tourist. One popular option is to take a guided tour of the volcano, which can include a visit to the Kilauea Visitor Center, a hike through the Thurston Lava Tube, and a visit to the Jaggar Museum. Other options include visiting the Pu'u 'O'o vent, where you can see the lava lake, or taking a boat tour to see the lava flows from the ocean.

It is important to note that Kilauea is a potentially dangerous place and visitors should always follow safety guidelines and listen to the instructions of their tour guides. It is also important to respect the cultural and natural resources of the area and to be mindful of the impact of tourism on the local community.

Hapuna Beach State Park

Hapuna Beach State Park is a popular tourist destination located on the Big Island of Hawaii. The park is known for its white sandy beach and crystal clear waters, which are ideal for swimming, snorkeling, and other beach activities.

Located on the sunny Kohala Coast, Hapuna Beach is one of the largest and most popular beaches on the Big Island. The beach stretches for over a mile and is surrounded by lush green lawns and palm trees, making it a perfect place to relax and soak up the sun. The beach is also great for surfing, bodyboarding, and other water sports.

In addition to the beach, Hapuna Beach State Park also offers several amenities and facilities for visitors, including restrooms, showers, and a large pavilion with picnic tables. There is also a lifeguard on duty to ensure the safety of swimmers.

The park is open from sunrise to sunset, and there is a small fee for parking. There are also a few nearby accommodations and restaurants for visitors who want to stay longer and explore the area.

Overall, Hapuna Beach State Park is a beautiful and popular tourist destination on the Big Island of Hawaii that offers a variety of activities and amenities for visitors to enjoy.

Mauna Loa

Mauna Loa is a shield volcano on the island of Hawaii, and it is one of the most popular tourist destinations in the state. Here are some things that tourists might do while visiting Mauna Loa:

Hike to the summit: Mauna Loa is the world's largest volcano in terms of mass, and it has a distinctive shape with a broad, gently sloping profile. There are several trails that lead to the summit, which stands at an elevation of 13,679 feet (4,170 meters). The hike can be challenging due to the high altitude and the rocky terrain, so it is recommended for experienced hikers in good physical condition.

Visit the Mauna Loa Observatory: Located near the summit of the volcano, the Mauna Loa Observatory is a research facility run by the National Oceanic and Atmospheric Administration (NOAA). It is dedicated to studying the Earth's atmosphere and climate, and it is open to the public for guided tours.

Take a scenic drive: The Mauna Loa Scenic Byway is a scenic drive that circles the base of the volcano and offers spectacular views of the surrounding landscape. The byway is about 60 miles (97 kilometers) long and takes about 3 hours to complete.

Explore the Mauna Loa Rainforest: The rainforest around Mauna Loa is home to a diverse array of plant and animal life, including many endemic species that are found nowhere else on Earth. Visitors can take guided tours of the rainforest, or explore on their own using hiking trails.

Learn about Hawaiian culture: Mauna Loa is an important cultural site for the native Hawaiian people, and there are many opportunities for tourists to learn about Hawaiian culture and history while visiting the area. This might include visiting cultural centers, participating in cultural activities, or visiting historic sites.

Waipio Valley

Waipio Valley is a valley located on the island of Hawaii in the state of Hawaii. It is located on the northeastern side of the island, about 25 miles northwest of Hilo. The valley is known for its beautiful and remote location, and it is a popular tourist destination for those interested in the natural beauty of Hawaii.

Here are some of the main attractions and activities in Waipio Valley:

Hiking: The Waipio Valley Lookout offers stunning views of the valley and the surrounding landscape, and there are several trails leading down into the valley for those who want to explore on foot.

Horseback Riding: Guided horseback riding tours are available in the valley, allowing visitors to experience the beauty of the valley from the back of a horse.

Waterfalls: The valley is home to several beautiful waterfalls, including Hiilawe Falls, which is one of the tallest waterfalls in Hawaii.

Beach: Waipio Valley Beach is a black sand beach located at the bottom of the valley. It is a popular spot for swimming and surfing, although the waves can be very powerful and are not recommended for inexperienced swimmers.

Cultural Experiences: Waipio Valley is home to a small Hawaiian community, and there are several cultural experiences available for visitors, including taro farming tours and Hawaiian cultural demonstrations.

Scenic Drives: The drive from Hilo to Waipio Valley offers beautiful views of the coastline and the surrounding landscape, and it is a popular attraction in itself.

Rainbow Falls

Rainbow Falls is a popular tourist destination in Hilo, Hawaii, located on the Big Island. The waterfall gets its name from the rainbow that is often seen in the mist of the falls when the sun is shining. The falls are located on the Wailuku River and are 80 feet tall.

To get to Rainbow Falls, you can either drive or take a tour from Hilo. There is a small parking lot at the falls, but it can fill up quickly, so it's best to arrive early in the morning to ensure a spot. From the parking lot, it's a short walk to the falls, which are located in a park called Wailuku River State Park.

There is a viewing platform at the base of the falls, where you can get a good view of the falls and the rainbow that often appears in the mist. There is also a hiking trail that leads to the top of the falls, which offers a different perspective on the falls and the surrounding area.

While visiting Rainbow Falls, you should also take the time to explore the rest of Hilo and the Big Island. There are many other attractions in the area, including the Mauna Kea Observatory, the Hawaii Tropical Botanical Garden, and the Akaka Falls State Park.

Akaka Falls State Park

Akaka Falls State Park is a state park located on the island of Hawaii in the US state of Hawaii. The park is known for its beautiful scenery, including Akaka Falls, a waterfall that drops 442 feet (135 meters) into a lush green gorge.

Some popular tourist attractions and activities at Akaka Falls State Park include:

Hiking: The park has a number of hiking trails that take visitors through the park's dense rainforest and past several waterfalls, including Akaka Falls.

Sightseeing: The park is a great place to take in the natural beauty of Hawaii, with its cascading waterfalls, lush vegetation, and colorful tropical flowers.

Photography: The park's stunning landscapes and waterfalls make it a popular spot for photographers.

Picnicking: The park has several picnic areas where visitors can enjoy a meal while taking in the beauty of the park.

Swimming: Some visitors like to cool off in the park's swimming holes, which are located near the falls.

Overall, Akaka Falls State Park is a great place to spend a day enjoying the natural beauty of Hawaii.

Pololu Valley Lookout

Pololu Valley Lookout is a scenic overlook on the island of Hawaii, located in the northern part of the island on the Hamakua Coast. The lookout offers breathtaking views of the Pololu Valley and the Pacific Ocean.

Visitors to Pololu Valley Lookout can take in the stunning views of the valley and ocean from the overlook, which is located at the end of a winding road that leads down from the top of a ridge. The overlook is accessible by car or on foot, and there is a small parking area at the top of the ridge for those who choose to drive.

In addition to enjoying the views from the overlook, visitors can also take a short hike down into the valley to explore the area further. The hike down to the valley floor is about a half mile long and takes about 20-30 minutes to complete. The trail is relatively easy and well-maintained, but it does involve some steep sections and can be slippery when wet, so visitors should take care when hiking.

Once at the bottom of the valley, visitors can explore the lush, green landscape and take in the beauty of the surrounding waterfalls and streams. The valley is home to a wide variety of plant and animal life, and it is a popular spot for birdwatching.

Other activities in the area include swimming in the ocean, which is accessible from the valley floor and visiting the nearby town of Hawi, which offers a variety of shopping and dining options.

Overall, Pololu Valley Lookout is a beautiful and peaceful spot that offers visitors the opportunity to take in the natural beauty of the island of Hawaii. It is a great place to spend an afternoon exploring and enjoying the outdoors.

Ka Lae

Ka Lae, also known as South Point, is a location on the Big Island of Hawaii known for its rich history and cultural significance. It is located at the southernmost point of the island and is the southernmost point in the United States.

There are several notable attractions and activities in Ka Lae that tourists can enjoy. One of the main attractions is the South Point Cliff, which offers breathtaking views of the surrounding ocean and coastline. Tourists can also visit the South Point Lighthouse, which was built in the late 1800s and is now a popular spot for photography.

In addition to these attractions, there are several outdoor activities that tourists can enjoy in Ka Lae. These include hiking, fishing, and snorkeling in the crystal-clear waters surrounding the area. Visitors can also participate in traditional Hawaiian activities such as spearfishing and exploring the many cultural and historical sites located in the area.

Overall, Ka Lae is a beautiful and culturally significant location that offers a variety of activities and attractions for tourists to enjoy. Whether you are interested in history, culture, or outdoor adventure, Ka Lae has something for everyone.

Kona Coast

The Kona Coast is a region on the west side of the island of Hawaii. It is known for its sunny weather, beautiful beaches, and cultural and historical sites.

Some popular activities for tourists visiting the Kona Coast include:

Swimming and snorkeling: The Kona Coast is home to some of the best snorkeling and diving spots in the world, with crystal-clear waters and abundant marine life.

Surfing: The Kona Coast is also a popular destination for surfers, with year-round waves and a number of breaks suitable for beginners and experienced surfers alike.

Hiking: The island of Hawaii has many trails that offer stunning views of the coast and the surrounding landscape. The Kona Coast is home to several trails that range from easy to challenging, including the Kona Hema Preserve and the Pu'u Wa'awa'a State Wayside.

Cultural activities: The Kona Coast is home to a number of cultural and historical sites, including the Pu'uhonua o Honaunau National Historical Park, which is a place of refuge for ancient Hawaiians, and the Hulihee Palace, a historic summer home for Hawaiian royalty.

Golf: The Kona Coast is home to several world-class golf courses, including the Mauna Kea Golf Course and the Makani Golf Club.

Shopping and dining: The Kona Coast is home to a number of shopping and dining options, ranging from local markets and artisanal shops to upscale restaurants and cafes.

Whale watching: During the winter months, the Kona Coast is a great place to go whale watching, as the region is home to a number of migratory humpback whales.

Stargazing: The Kona Coast is known for its clear night skies, making it a great place to stargaze and view constellations and planets.

There are many other activities and attractions to enjoy on the Kona Coast, including visiting coffee farms, exploring botanical gardens, and attending cultural events and festivals.

CHAPTER 5

Top 10 Must Try Best Local Cuisine

Hawaii is a melting pot of cultural influences, and this is reflected in its cuisine. Many traditional Hawaiian dishes are a blend of flavors and techniques from various cultures, including Polynesian, Japanese, Chinese, Filipino, Korean, and Portuguese.

Hawaii Shave Ice

Shave ice is a popular treat in Hawaii that is made by shaving a block of ice into fine, fluffy flakes and topping it with a variety of sweet syrups. It is similar to a snow cone, but the ice is much finer and softer, and the syrups are typically fruit-flavored and more intensely flavored than the syrups used on snow cones.

Shave ice is a popular refreshment for tourists and locals alike in Hawaii, and it can be found at stands and kiosks all over the islands. It is often served in a paper cone or cup and topped with a variety of syrups, such as cherry, pineapple, mango, and coconut. Some stands also offer a variety of toppings, such as ice cream, mochi (a Japanese rice cake), and azuki beans.

Shave ice is a refreshing and satisfying treat that is perfect for beating the heat in Hawaii. It is a must-try for any visitor to the islands, and it is an integral part of the local food culture.

Spam musubi

Spam musubi is a popular snack in Hawaii that consists of a slice of grilled Spam placed on top of a block of rice, which is then wrapped with a strip of seaweed (nori). The snack is believed to have originated in Hawaii during World War II when Spam became a common food item for soldiers stationed on the islands. It is now a staple food in Hawaii and can be found at most convenience stores, supermarkets, and snack shops throughout the state.

In addition to being a popular snack, Spam musubi has also become a symbol of Hawaiian culture and is often served at local events and festivals. Many tourists visiting Hawaii also enjoy trying Spam musubi and other local dishes as a way to experience the unique food culture of the islands.

Hawaii Sushi

Hawaii is known for its diverse and vibrant culture, which includes a unique blend of Asian and Western influences. One of the ways this is reflected in the local cuisine is through the popularity of sushi in Hawaii. Sushi, a Japanese dish made with vinegared rice and various toppings such as raw fish or vegetables, has become a popular choice for both locals and tourists in Hawaii.

There are many sushi restaurants to choose from in Hawaii, ranging from traditional Japanese sushi bars to more casual and modern eateries. Some popular local variations of sushi include poke bowls, which are bowls of diced raw fish mixed with vegetables and seasonings, and spam musubi.

In addition to traditional sushi restaurants, you can also find sushi being served at food trucks, farmer's markets, and other casual dining locations throughout the islands. Whether you're looking for a fancy dinner out or a quick and convenient meal on the go, you'll be able to find delicious sushi in Hawaii.

Haupia

Haupia is a traditional Hawaiian dessert made from coconut milk and cornstarch or arrowroot. It is often served in a jelly-like consistency and has a creamy, coconut flavor. Haupia is a popular treat in Hawaii and can be found at many restaurants and food stands throughout the islands. It is often served as a topping for cakes or as a filling for pastries, and can also be enjoyed on its own as a refreshing and satisfying snack.

There are many variations in the recipe for haupia, but the most common method involves mixing coconut milk, sugar, cornstarch, or arrowroot together in a saucepan. The mixture is heated until it thickens and then poured into a dish to set. Once it has been set, it can be cut into squares or other shapes and served. Some variations of the recipe may include the addition of flavors such as vanilla or pineapple, or the inclusion of other ingredients such as coconut cream or shredded coconut.

Haupia has a long history in Hawaiian culture and is often served at special occasions such as weddings and luau parties. It is a beloved treat that is enjoyed by people of all ages and is a staple of Hawaiian cuisine. If you are visiting Hawaii and have the opportunity to try haupia, it is definitely worth a taste!

Poke

Poke is a traditional Hawaiian dish that typically consists of diced raw fish (such as tuna or salmon) mixed with a variety of seasonings and other ingredients, such as onions, seaweed, and sesame seeds. It is often served over rice or as a topping for salads.

The Big Island is home to a variety of poke shops and restaurants that serve this popular dish. If you are a tourist visiting the Big Island, you may be able to find poke at a variety of local markets, supermarkets, and food trucks, as well as at sit-down restaurants.

Poke is a popular choice for tourists visiting the Big Island due to its flavorful, refreshing taste and its convenient, portable nature. It is often served as a quick and easy meal or snack that can be enjoyed on the go.

If you are interested in trying poke while visiting the Big Island, you may want to ask locals or your hotel or vacation rental staff for recommendations on where to find the best poke. You can also look for poke shops or restaurants in your area using online directories or apps.

Chicken Katsu

Chicken katsu is a popular dish in Hawaii that consists of breaded and fried chicken cutlets, often served with a tonkatsu sauce and rice. It is often served at local plate lunch restaurants, as well as at food trucks and other casual dining establishments on the island of Hawaii.

To make chicken katsu, chicken breasts are typically pounded to an even thickness and then coated in a mixture of flour, egg, and breadcrumbs before being fried in oil until crispy and golden brown. The chicken is then sliced into thin cutlets and served over rice, often with a side of tonkatsu sauce for dipping.

In addition to being a popular menu item at local restaurants, chicken katsu is also a popular choice for tourists visiting the island of Hawaii, as it is a relatively affordable and satisfying meal that can be found at a variety of dining establishments.

Overall, chicken katsu is a delicious and popular dish that is well worth trying if you are visiting the island of Hawaii.

Grilled Teriyaki Chicken

Big Island Grilled Teriyaki Chicken is a popular dish that originated in Hawaii. It is made with marinated chicken grilled and served with a sweet teriyaki sauce. The marinade consists of sugar, soy sauce, garlic, ginger, and sesame oil, which provides the dish with its signature sweet and savory flavor. The chicken is cooked on an open flame, giving it a unique smoky flavor. The addition of pineapple and bell peppers to the marinade, as well as the grill marks, adds a delightful texture and flavor to the dish. Big Island Grilled Teriyaki Chicken is often served with white rice or macaroni salad and is a popular dish for tourists visiting Hawaii.

Mochi

Mochi is a type of traditional Hawaiian dessert. It is made by pounding cooked sweet rice into a paste, then rolling it into balls and wrapping it in a banana leaf. The balls are typically filled with sweetened fruits, such as pineapple, mango, or coconut. Mochi Hawaii is often served as a snack or dessert at luau parties, and it can also be found in some restaurants, bakeries, and grocery stores. The dessert is a popular treat among both locals and visitors alike.

Coconut Rice

One of the most popular dishes in Hawaii is coconut rice, which is a delicious and flavorful combination of coconut milk, white rice, and fresh vegetables.

Coconut rice is a traditional dish served in many homes across Hawaii and is often served as a side dish with fish, chicken, pork, or vegetables. Coconut rice is usually prepared in a pot on the stove, where the coconut milk and white rice are first cooked together. Then, vegetables such as carrots, peas, and mushrooms are added to the pot and cooked until the vegetables are tender.

This dish can be served plain, or it can be garnished with fried shallots or onions, cilantro, and lime juice. It is also a great accompaniment to dishes such as teriyaki chicken, fish tacos, and pork chops. Coconut rice is often served as a main dish as well, with a simple stir-fry of vegetables, or with a variety of seafood.

Coconut rice is a great way to experience the unique flavors of Hawaii. Whether you are visiting for a vacation or just looking to try something new, this traditional dish is sure to be a hit.

Hawaii Spam Fried Rice

Hawaii Spam fried rice is a popular dish in Hawaii, which is a combination of two of the island state's most iconic foods – Spam (a canned processed meat product) and fried rice. This dish was created by the local plantation workers, who were looking for a way to make the canned Spam more interesting and flavorful.

Hawaii Spam fried rice typically consists of cooked white or brown rice, Spam (usually cubed or sliced), vegetables such as onion, scallions, celery, carrots and peas, garlic, and seasonings such as soy sauce, fish sauce, and sesame oil. The dish is usually cooked in a large wok over high heat. The vegetables are added first and cooked for a few minutes before the Spam is added. The cooked Spam is then mixed in with the vegetables and the cooked rice is added. The dish is then cooked for a few more minutes until the ingredients are well mixed and the rice is lightly browned.

Hawaii Spam fried rice is often served as a side dish, but it can also be served as a main dish with a side of vegetables or salad. It is a popular dish among tourists, as it is a quick and easy way

In addition to these traditional dishes, Hawaii is also home to a wide variety of international cuisines, including, Thai, and Italian, which have all had a significant influence on the local food culture.

CHAPTER 6

Big Island Weather

The Big Island, also known as Hawaii Island, is the largest of the Hawaiian Islands and is located in the tropical zone. It has a diverse range of climates and weather patterns due to its size and location, so it's important to be prepared for a range of weather conditions.

The weather on the Big Island can vary significantly depending on the location and elevation. The island has several distinct climate zones, ranging from dry and arid to wet and tropical.

The western and southern parts of the island, including Kailua-Kona and Waikoloa, have a dry and sunny climate, with temperatures ranging from the mid-70s to low 80s Fahrenheit (around 25-30°C) throughout the year. These areas are prone to drought and can be quite hot and humid during the summer months.

The eastern and northern parts of the island, including Hilo and Volcano, have a more tropical climate, with higher humidity and more frequent rainfall. The temperatures in these areas are generally cooler, ranging from the mid-70s to mid-80s Fahrenheit (around 25-30°C) throughout the year. The rainforest areas in this part of the island can be quite wet, with up to 240 inches of rain per year.

The Big Island is also home to the Mauna Kea and Mauna Loa volcanoes, which are located at high elevations and can be very cold and windy, with temperatures dropping below freezing at night. It's important to dress warmly if you plan to visit these areas.

The weather on the Big Island of Hawaii can vary greatly depending on which part of the island you are visiting and the time of year. Here is a general overview of the weather on the Big Island from January to December:

January

January is usually the driest month on the Big Island, with temperatures ranging from the mid-70s to mid-80s Fahrenheit (24-29°C) during the day and cooler temperatures at night. The Hilo side of the island tends to be wetter and cooler, with temperatures in the mid-to-upper 70s Fahrenheit (24-26°C) and higher humidity. The Kona side of the island tends to be drier and warmer, with temperatures in the low to mid-80s Fahrenheit (28-29°C).

February

February is similar to January, with dry conditions and temperatures ranging from the mid-60s to mid-80s Fahrenheit during the day and cooler temperatures at night.

March

March is typically the beginning of the wet season on the Big Island, with more frequent showers and higher humidity. Temperatures range from the mid-70s to mid-80s Fahrenheit during the day and cooler temperatures at night.

April

April is typically the wettest month on the Big Island, with frequent showers and higher humidity. Temperatures range from the mid-70s to mid-80s

Fahrenheit during the day and cooler temperatures at night.

May

May is typically the transition month between the wet and dry seasons on the Big Island, with showers becoming less frequent and humidity decreasing. Temperatures range from the mid-70s to mid-80s Fahrenheit during the day and cooler temperatures at night.

June

June is typically the beginning of the dry season on the Big Island, with fewer showers and lower humidity. Temperatures range from the mid-70s to mid-80s Fahrenheit during the day and cooler temperatures at night.

July

July is similar to June, with dry conditions and temperatures ranging from the mid-70s to mid-80s Fahrenheit during the day and cooler temperatures at night.

August

August is typically the hottest month on the Big Island, with temperatures ranging from the mid-70s to mid-80s Fahrenheit during the day and cooler temperatures at night.

September

September is similar to August, with warm temperatures and dry conditions. Temperatures range from the mid-70s to mid-80s Fahrenheit during the day and cooler temperatures at night.

October

October is typically the transition month between the dry and wet seasons on the Big Island, with showers becoming more frequent and humidity increasing.

Temperatures range from the mid-70s to mid-80s Fahrenheit during the day and cooler temperatures at night.

November

November is typically the wettest month on the Big Island, with frequent showers and higher humidity. Temperatures range from the mid-70s to mid-80s Fahrenheit during the day and cooler temperatures at night.

December: December is similar to November, with wet conditions and temperatures ranging from the mid-70s to mid-80s Fahrenheit during the day and cooler temperatures at night.

It is important to note that the weather on the Big Island can vary significantly from year to year, and these are just general averages.

CHAPTER 7

Best Time to Visit Big Island

The best time to visit the Big Island of Hawaii depends on what you want to do and see while you're there. Here are some things to consider when visiting:

Weather

The western and southern parts of the island tend to be drier and sunnier, while the eastern and northern parts tend to be wetter and cloudier.

Crowds

The Big Island is the least visited of the Hawaiian Islands, so it tends to be less crowded than Oahu or Maui. However, the island does get more crowded during peak tourist season, which runs from December to April.

Activities

The Big Island is known for its diverse range of activities, including snorkeling, surfing, hiking, and exploring volcanoes. If you're interested in these activities, you may want to visit during the drier months of the year, which tend to be from April to October.

Overall, the best time to visit the Big Island is probably from April to October, when the weather is drier and the crowds are smaller. However, the island is beautiful and has plenty to offer year-round, so if you can't visit during those months, you can still have a great time.

CHAPTER 8

Big Island Traveling Essentials

When planning a vacation to the Big Island of Hawaii, there are a few essential items that you should consider packing. Here is a list of some of the most important items to bring with you on your trip:

Sunscreen: The sun in Hawaii can be intense, especially at higher elevations or during the summer months. Be sure to pack plenty of sunscreen with a high SPF to protect your skin from sunburn.

Beach gear: If you plan on spending time at the beach, you'll want to bring beach towels, swimsuits, sandals, and hats to keep you comfortable in the sun.

Insect repellent: Mosquitoes and other insects can be a problem in certain parts of the island, especially in areas with standing water. Pack insect repellent to keep these pests at bay.

Light, comfortable clothing: The weather in Hawaii is generally warm and humid, so it's best to pack lightweight, breathable clothing that will keep you comfortable in the heat.

Rain gear: Even though the Big Island is known for its sunny weather, it's always a good idea to pack a rain jacket or umbrella in case of unexpected showers.

Camera: The Big Island is home to some of the most beautiful landscapes in the world, so don't forget to bring a camera to capture all of the amazing sights you'll see during your trip.

Snacks and water: It's always a good idea to bring some snacks and bottled water with you, especially if you plan on doing any hiking or other outdoor activities.

First aid kit: It's always a good idea to have a basic first aid kit on hand when traveling, just in case of any minor emergencies.

Money: Make sure you have enough cash or credit cards to cover any expenses you might incur during your trip.

Big Island Hiking Packing

When packing for a hike on the Big Island of Hawaii, it's important to be prepared for a range of weather conditions and terrain. Here are some well-known guidelines for what to bring:

Bag pack: It is always a good idea to carry a backpack so all your hiking needs will be fitted in it.

Water: It's essential to stay hydrated while hiking, so be sure to bring plenty of water. A good rule of thumb is to bring at least one liter of water per hour of hiking.

Food: Pack snacks or a lunch to sustain your energy on the trail. High-energy snacks like nuts, granola bars, and jerky can be helpful.

Clothing: Wear comfortable, breathable clothing that will help you regulate your body temperature. Pack a light rain jacket, as the weather on the Big Island can be unpredictable. Consider Bringing sunscreen and a hat to protect your skin from the sun.

Footwear: Wear sturdy, comfortable shoes or boots that offer good support and traction.

First aid kit: It's always a good idea to bring a basic first aid kit on any hike, including items like band-aids, antiseptic wipes, and any prescription medications you may need.

Maps and a compass: Bring a map of the trail you'll be hiking and a compass in case you get lost.

Emergency whistle: A whistle can be useful in attracting attention if you need help.

Headlamp or flashlight: If you plan to be out on the trail after dark, bring a light source.

Trash bag: Leave no trace by packing out all of your trash, including food wrappers and water bottles.

Big Island Dive Snorkel Packing

When preparing for a diving or snorkeling trip to the Big Island of Hawaii, there are a few key items that you will want to make sure to bring with you.

Dive or snorkel gear: This includes a mask, fins, snorkel, and either a wetsuit or a dive skin, depending on the water temperature. If you don't own your own gear, you can typically rent it from a local dive shop.

Sun protection: The Big Island gets plenty of sunshine, so be sure to bring sunscreen, a hat, and sunglasses to protect yourself from the sun's harmful rays.

Beach towels and swimsuit: You'll want to bring a couple of towels to dry off after diving or snorkeling, and a swimsuit to wear while you're in the water.

Water and snacks: It's important to stay hydrated and nourished while you're out on the water, so bring plenty of water and some snacks to keep you going.

Camera: If you want to capture your diving or snorkeling experiences, be sure to bring a waterproof camera or waterproof housing for your regular camera.

First aid kit: It's always a good idea to bring a small first aid kit with you, in case of any minor injuries or emergencies.

Cash or credit card: You may want to bring some cash or a credit card to pay for any additional gear or services that you might need while on your trip.

Water shoes: Depending on where you'll be diving or snorkeling, you may want to bring a pair of water shoes to protect your feet from sharp rocks or coral.

Big Island Golf Packing

There are a few key things to consider when golf packing:

Clothing: Pack comfortable, lightweight clothing that is appropriate for the weather and climate of your destination. This may include shorts, t-shirts, and a light jacket or rain gear if needed.

Golf clubs: Make sure you have all of the clubs you need for your round, including a driver, woods, irons, wedges, and putter. Consider using a travel cover or bag to protect your clubs during transport.

Golf shoes: Pack a pair of golf shoes that are comfortable and provide good traction on the course.

Golf balls: Pack plenty of golf balls, as you may lose some during your round.

Tees: Bring a supply of tees to use on the course.

Gloves: Pack a golf glove to help improve your grip on the club.

Other equipment: Consider packing other equipment such as a rangefinder, GPS device, or a towel to clean your clubs and balls.

Big Island Beach Packing

Packing for a trip to the Big Island of Hawaii can be a fun and exciting experience, but it's important to make sure you have everything you need for your stay. Here is a list of items you may want to consider packing for a beach trip to the Big Island:

Sunscreen: The sun in Hawaii is strong, so it's important to protect your skin with a high SPF sunscreen.

Beach towels: Pack at least two towels per person, one for drying off and one for laying on.

Beach chairs or a beach umbrella: These will provide a comfortable spot to relax and enjoy the beach.

Beach games: Pack items like a frisbee or beach ball to have some fun in the sun.

Snacks and drinks: Pack plenty of water and some snacks like fruit, crackers, or granola bars to keep you fueled up while at the beach.

Hats and sunglasses: These will help protect your face and eyes from the sun.

Rash guard or swim shirt: If you're planning on snorkeling or surfing, a rash guard or swim shirt can help protect your skin from the sun and from abrasions caused by the board or equipment.

Beach bag: A bag with a sturdy strap will be helpful for carrying all of your beach items.

Beach cover-up: A cover-up or lightweight shirt and shorts can be useful for covering up after a day in the sun.

Sandals or water shoes: These will protect your feet from the hot sand and can also be useful for activities like snorkeling.

Camera: Don't forget to bring a camera to capture all of your memories from your beach trip on the Big Island!

It's also a good idea to check the forecast and pack accordingly. If it's going to be hot and sunny, pack lightweight, breathable clothing. If it's going to be cooler or rainy, pack layers and a rain jacket. And don't forget to bring your swimsuit, of course!

By packing these items, you'll be well prepared for a great adventure on the Big Island of Hawaii.

CHAPTER 9

Big Island Accommodation Options

The Big Island of Hawaii is home to a wide range of accommodation options, including resorts, hotels, vacation rentals, and bed and breakfasts.

Resorts on the Big Island range from luxury properties with golf courses, spas, and a range of amenities, to more modest properties that offer a more laid-back atmosphere. Many resorts are located along the coast and offer access to beaches, water sports, and other outdoor activities.

Hotels on the Big Island can range from budget-friendly options to more upscale properties. Many hotels are located in the island's main tourist areas, such as Kailua-Kona and Hilo, and offer a variety of amenities, such as pools, fitness centers, and restaurants.

Vacation rentals on the Big Island include options such as vacation homes, condos, and cottages. These properties offer the privacy and convenience of a home and are often located in residential areas or in more rural parts of the island.

Bed and breakfasts on the Big Island offer a more intimate and personalized experience, with owners often living on the property and providing a home-cooked breakfast each morning. These properties are often located in residential areas and offer a more laid-back atmosphere.

5 Best Budget places to stay on Big Island

Here are 5 budget-friendly places to stay on the Big Island of Hawaii:

Kona Coast Resort - This resort is located in the heart of Kona and offers a variety of room types, including studios, one-bedroom, and two-bedroom units. The resort has a pool, hot tub, and barbecue grills, and is located near shopping, dining, and recreational activities.

Phone number: (808) 324-1721

Hilo Seaside Hotel - This hotel is located in Hilo and offers basic rooms with private balconies, as well as a pool, hot tub, and outdoor grills. The hotel is located near Hilo Bay and is close to shopping and dining options.
Phone number: (808) 935-0821

Waikoloa Beach Marriott Resort & Spa - This resort is located on the Kohala Coast and offers a variety of room types, including standard rooms, studios, and one-bedroom suites. The resort has multiple pools, a hot tub, and a variety of dining and recreational options.

Phone number: (808) 886-6789

Hilton Waikoloa Village - This resort is located on the Kohala Coast and offers a variety of room types, including standard rooms, studios, and one-bedroom suites. The resort has multiple pools, a hot tub, and a variety of dining and recreational options.

Phone number: (808) 886-1234

Mauna Kea Beach Hotel - This hotel is located on the Kohala Coast and offers a variety of room types, including standard rooms, studios, and one-bedroom suites. The hotel has a pool, hot tub, and access to a private beach.

Phone number: (808) 882-7222

5 Best luxurious places to stay on Big Island

Here are five luxurious places to stay on the Big Island of Hawaii, along with their phone numbers:

Four Seasons Resort Hualalai - Located on the Kona-Kohala Coast, this resort offers luxury accommodations and amenities such as multiple pools, a spa, and golf courses.

Phone number: (808) 325-8000

Mauna Lani Bay Hotel & Bungalows - This luxury resort is located on the Kohala Coast and features multiple pools, a golf course, and a spa.

Phone number: (808) 885-6622

Fairmont Orchid, Hawaii - Located on the Kohala Coast, this luxury resort features multiple pools, a spa, and a golf course.

Phone number: (808) 885-2000

Hilton Waikoloa Village - Located on the Kohala Coast, this luxury resort features multiple pools, a water park, a spa, and a golf course.

Phone number: (808) 886-1234

Waikoloa Beach Marriott Resort & Spa - Located on the Kohala Coast, this luxury resort features multiple pools, a spa, and a golf course.

Phone number: (808) 886-6789

These resorts offer a range of luxurious accommodations and amenities, including spacious guest rooms, fine dining options, and recreational activities such as golf and spa services. They are all located on the Kohala Coast, which is known for its beautiful beaches and luxurious resorts.

Note: Include "+1" if you are calling outside of the United States.

CHAPTER 10

Traveling Itinerary

The Big Island of Hawaii is the largest and most diverse of the Hawaiian Islands. There are many things to see and do on the Big Island, so it's helpful to plan an itinerary to make the most of your visit. Here are some suggestions for things to include in your itinerary:

Big island 1-week Itinerary and Activities

There is so much to see and do on the Big Island of Hawaii, it can be tough to narrow it down to just one week! Here is a possible itinerary that covers some of the island's most popular attractions and activities:

Day 1

Arrive on the island and spend the day relaxing and getting settled in.
Consider taking a leisurely drive around the island to get a feel for the layout and see some of the beautiful scenery.

Day 2
Visit Hawaii Volcanoes National Park, which is home to two of the world's most active volcanoes, Kilauea and Mauna Loa. Take a guided tour of the park to learn about the geology and natural history of the area, and see steam vents, lava tubes, and other volcanic features.
In the evening, head to the town of Hilo and check out the Mokupapapa Discovery Center, which has interactive exhibits on the island's marine life and cultural history.

Day 3
Spend the day exploring the island's beautiful beaches and snorkeling spots. Some of the best places to visit include Hapuna Beach State Park, Anaeho'omalu Bay, and Kahaluu Beach Park.

Day 4
Take a trip to the island's western coast and visit the scenic Waipi'o Valley, which is known for its rugged beauty and secluded black sand beach. You can hike down into the valley or take a guided tour by ATV or horseback.

Day 5
Head to the island's northern tip and visit Pu'uhonua O Honaunau National Historical Park,

which is home to ancient Hawaiian temples and other cultural sites. Take a guided tour to learn about the island's rich history and traditions.

Day 6
Spend the day on the island's eastern coast, where you can visit the town of Pahoa and check out the Puna Coast Dive & Surf shop, which offers guided snorkeling and scuba diving trips. You can also visit the Ahalanui Hot Ponds, which are heated by underground volcanic vents.

Day 7
Take a scenic drive along the Saddle Road, which crosses the island from east to west, and visit Mauna Kea, the highest point on the island at 13,796 feet above sea level. You can take a guided tour of the observatories at the summit or just enjoy the incredible views from the visitor's center.

Big island 2 weeks Itinerary, Activities to do, and Food to eat

Here is a potential two-week itinerary for your trip, with some suggestions for things to do and food to try:

Day 1

Arrive on the Big Island and get settled in your accommodation.

In the evening, head to Kailua-Kona for a sunset walk along the waterfront and dinner at a local restaurant. Try some Hawaiian specialties like poke, Lau Lau (pork wrapped in taro leaves), or kalua pig (slow-roasted pork).

Day 2

Spend the day exploring the island's beautiful beaches. Head to Hapuna Beach State Park for a day of swimming, snorkeling, and sunbathing.

In the evening, dine at a local seafood restaurant and try some fresh catch of the day.

Day 3

Take a drive to the island's eastern coast and visit the Hawaii Volcanoes National Park. Hike through the park and see the active Kilauea volcano.

In the evening, have dinner at a restaurant in Hilo and try some local favorites like poi (mashed taro root), Lomi Lomi salmon (marinated salmon), and haupia (coconut milk pudding).

Day 4

Head to the north shore of the island and visit the Waipio Valley Lookout. Take a guided tour of the valley or hike down to the black sand beach.
In the evening, have dinner at a local restaurant and try some Hawaiian barbecue or teriyaki chicken.

Day 5

Spend the day exploring the island's unique botanical gardens. Visit the Hawaii Tropical Botanical Garden and the Onomea Bay Scenic Drive.
In the evening, dine at a local restaurant and try some Hawaiian-style sushi or tempura shrimp.

Day 6

Take a boat tour of the island's west coast and visit the historic Kealakekua Bay. Snorkel in the bay and see a variety of colorful tropical fish.
In the evening, have dinner at a local restaurant and try some Hawaiian-style poke bowls or grilled mahi-mahi.

Day 7

Head to the south shore of the island and visit the Pu'uhonua o Honaunau National Historical Park.

Take a guided tour of the park and learn about the island's history and culture.
In the evening, dine at a local restaurant and try a Hawaiian-style plate lunch (a combination of meat, rice, and macaroni salad).

Day 8
Take a drive to the island's northwest coast and visit Waimea Bay. Relax your body on the beach or Swim in the bay.
In the evening, have dinner at a local restaurant and try some Hawaiian-style sushi rolls or grilled ahi tuna.

Day 9
Spend the day exploring the island's waterfalls. Visit the Akaka Falls State Park and the Rainbow Falls State Park.
In the evening, have dinner at a local restaurant and try some Hawaiian-style shrimp scampi or grilled Mahi-Mahi.

Day 10
Take a boat tour of the island's east coast and visit the Captain Cook Monument. Snorkel in the waters off the coast and see a variety of tropical fish.
In the evening, dine at a local restaurant and try some Hawaiian-style grilled chicken or teriyaki beef.

Day 11
Activity: Visit the home of King Kamehameha
Food: Enjoy a traditional luau feast

Day 12
Activity: Take a tour of the Pu'uhonua O Honaunau National Historical Park
Food: Enjoy a seafood dinner at a local restaurant

Day 13
Activity: Take a tour of the Kohala Coast
Food: Enjoy a seafood dinner at a local restaurant

Day 14
Activity: Take a tour of the Panaewa Rainforest Zoo
Food: Enjoy a tropical lunch at the zoo's cafe

No matter what you decide to do on the Big Island, be sure to allow plenty of time to relax and enjoy the island's laid-back vibe.

CHAPTER 11

Big Island Tourist Safety Tips

Hawaii is generally a safe destination for tourists, but it's always a good idea to take precautions to ensure a safe and enjoyable trip.

Here are some safety tips for tourists visiting Hawaii:

Familiarize yourself with the local hazards: Hawaii has some unique hazards, such as high surf, strong currents, and volcanic activity. Be sure to research and understand these hazards before visiting, and follow all safety warnings and recommendations.

Stay hydrated: Hawaii's warm, humid climate can lead to dehydration if you're not careful. Be sure to drink plenty of water, especially if you're participating in activities that involve physical exertion.

Protect yourself from the sun: Hawaii's sunny climate means that you need to take precautions to protect your skin from the sun's harmful rays. Wear sunscreen with a high SPF, a hat, and sunglasses, and seek shade whenever possible.

Be mindful of your surroundings: As with any vacation destination, it's important to stay aware of your surroundings and to take precautions to protect yourself and your belongings. Avoid walking alone at night, and keep your valuables secure when you're out and about.

Know the local emergency numbers: In case of an emergency, it's important to know the local emergency numbers. In Hawaii, you can call 911 for emergencies, and (808) 935-3311. Non-emergency assistance.

Respect the local culture: Hawaii has a rich and diverse culture, and it's important to show respect for the customs and traditions of the local people. Be mindful of your behavior and actions, and be respectful of the local environment.

Purchase travel insurance: Travel insurance can provide peace of mind and financial protection in case of unexpected events such as trip cancellations, medical emergencies, or lost or stolen luggage. Consider purchasing travel insurance for your trip to Hawaii.

Keep valuables secure, such as by using a hotel safe or keeping them on your person.

If you're planning on participating in activities such as snorkeling, surfing, or hiking, make sure to follow all safety guidelines and use proper equipment.

By following these safety tips, you can help ensure a safe and enjoyable trip to Hawaii.

CHAPTER 12

Visiting Big Island on a Budget

Visiting the Big Island of Hawaii can be a wonderful and memorable experience, but it's important to plan and budget carefully to make the most of your trip. Here are some tips for visiting the Big Island on a budget:

Look for deals and discounts on flights and accommodations: There are often discounts available for flights to the Big Island, especially if you book in advance or travel during the off-season. Similarly, you can often find deals on hotels and vacation rentals by booking well in advance or being flexible with your dates.

Consider staying in a vacation rental or Airbnb: Vacation rentals and Airbnb properties can often be more cost-effective than hotels, especially if you are traveling with a group. These options also often offer more space and amenities than a traditional hotel room.

Eat local: Instead of dining at touristy restaurants, try eating at local markets and food trucks. These options are often more affordable and can provide a more authentic cultural experience.

Use public transportation: The Big Island has a public bus system that can be a cheap and convenient way to get around the island. Renting a car can be expensive, so consider using public transportation or car-sharing services to save money.

Look for free or low-cost activities: There are many free or low-cost activities to enjoy on the Big Island, such as visiting the beach, hiking, and exploring local parks and botanical gardens.

Consider traveling during the off-season, when prices for flights and accommodation are generally lower.

Look for package deals that include flights, accommodation, and activities, as these can sometimes be more cost-effective than booking everything separately.

Consider staying in a vacation rental or a more affordable hotel rather than a luxury resort.

Consider purchasing a CityPASS, which provides discounts on popular attractions and activities.

Plan activities in advance and purchase tickets online, as this can often be cheaper than buying tickets on the spot.

Consider purchasing a National Parks Pass, which allows for free entry to all national parks in the U.S. for a year. The Big Island has two national parks: Hawaii Volcanoes National Park and Pu'uhonua o Hōnaunau National Historical Park.

Avoid booking last minute, as prices are often higher for last-minute bookings.

By following these tips and being mindful of your budget, you can have a wonderful and affordable trip to the Big Island of Hawaii.

CHAPTER 13

Big Island Festival Events

There are many festivals and events held on the island throughout the year, which can vary in size, focus, and duration. Some festivals may be small and locally organized, while others may be larger and more well-known.

Festivals on the Big Island can focus on a variety of themes, such as cultural traditions, art, music, food, sports, and environmental issues. Many festivals are held outdoors and may involve activities such as parades, performances, and vendors selling food, crafts, and other items.

Some examples of festivals that might be held on the Big Island throughout the year include:

Kona Brewers Festival (March)

The Kona Brewers Festival is an annual event that takes place in Kona, Hawaii. The festival celebrates the art of brewing and features a variety of local and national craft beers. It also includes live music, food, and other entertainment. The festival is typically held in March and is a popular event among tourists and locals alike. It is a great opportunity to sample a wide range of craft beers and learn more about the brewing process. The festival also helps to support local breweries and the community.

Merrie Monarch Festival (April)

It is a celebration of Hawaiian culture and traditions, including hula dancing, music, and other cultural practices. The festival is named after King David Kalākaua, who was known as the "Merrie Monarch" for his promotion of Hawaiian culture and traditions during his reign in the late 1800s. The festival typically takes place in April and includes a variety of events, such as hula competitions, craft fairs, and concerts. It is a popular event among tourists and locals alike and attracts people from all over the world. The festival is also an opportunity to learn more about Hawaiian culture and traditions, and to experience the rich history of the islands.

Hawaii Food & Wine Festival (May)

The festival celebrates the diverse and unique food and wine culture of Hawaii and features a variety of local and international chefs, winemakers, and culinary experts. The festival typically takes place in the fall and includes a variety of events, such as culinary demonstrations, wine tastings, and gourmet dinners. It is a popular event among tourists and locals alike and attracts people from all over the world. The festival is a great opportunity to sample a wide range of delicious food and drink and to learn more about the culinary traditions of Hawaii. It is also an opportunity to support local food and drink producers and celebrate the rich culinary culture of the islands.

Kamehameha Festival (May)

The Kamehameha Festival is an annual event that takes place in honor of King Kamehameha the Great, who united the Hawaiian Islands under a single kingdom in the late 1700s. The festival typically takes place in June and includes a variety of events, such as cultural demonstrations, hula performances, and live music. It is a popular event among tourists and locals alike and is an opportunity to learn more about the history and culture of Hawaii. The festival also helps to celebrate and honor the legacy of King Kamehameha, who is an important figure in Hawaiian history. It is a time for people to come together and celebrate the rich culture and traditions of the islands.

Paniolo Parade & Ho'olaule'a (June)

The Paniolo Parade & Ho'olaule'a is an annual event that takes place on the island of Hawaii. The event is a celebration of the paniolo, or Hawaiian cowboy, culture, and traditions, and includes a parade, live music, and a variety of other activities. The parade typically takes place in the morning and features floats, marching bands, and other participants. The ho'olaule'a, or celebration, takes place in the afternoon and includes live music, food, and other entertainment. The event is a popular tourist attraction and is an opportunity to learn more about the paniolo culture and traditions, which have a rich history on the island of Hawaii. It is also a time for people to come together and celebrate the unique culture and history of the islands.

King Kamehameha Hula Competition (July)

The King Kamehameha Hula Competition is an annual event that takes place in Hilo, Hawaii. It is a hula competition that celebrates the art of hula and the rich cultural traditions of Hawaii. The competition is named after King Kamehameha the Great. The event typically takes place in June and includes solo and group hula competitions for both kahiko (ancient hula) and 'auana (modern hula) styles. It is a popular event among tourists and locals alike and attracts people from all over the world. The competition is an opportunity to learn more about the art of hula and the rich cultural traditions of Hawaii. It is also a time for hula practitioners to showcase their skills and pay tribute to the cultural traditions of the islands.

Pana'ewa Rainforest Zoo Ho'olaule'a (September)

The Pana'ewa Rainforest Zoo Ho'olaule'a is an annual event that takes place at the Pana'ewa Rainforest Zoo in Hilo, Hawaii. The event is a celebration of Hawaiian culture and features a variety of activities, such as live music, food, and cultural demonstrations. It typically takes place in the summer and is a popular event among tourists and locals alike. The Pana'ewa Rainforest Zoo Ho'olaule'a is an opportunity to learn more about Hawaiian culture and to experience the unique natural beauty of the Pana'ewa Rainforest. It is also a chance to support the zoo and its efforts to preserve and protect the rainforest and its diverse array of plant and animal life.

Ironman World Championship (October)

The Ironman World Championship is an annual triathlon event that takes place in Kailua-Kona, Hawaii. The event consists of a 2.4-mile (3.86 km) swim, a 112-mile (180.25 km) bike ride, and a 26.2-mile (42.2 km) marathon, and is considered one of the most challenging and prestigious triathlon events in the world. The Ironman World Championship attracts top athletes from around the globe and is a popular event among tourists and locals alike. The event typically takes place in October and is a celebration of the human spirit, determination, and endurance. It is an opportunity for athletes to test their limits and for spectators to witness the incredible feats of athleticism and determination of the competitors. The Ironman World Championship is also a major economic and cultural event for the island of Hawaii and attracts thousands of people to the region each year.

Kona Coffee Cultural Festival (November)

The Kona Coffee Cultural Festival is an annual event that takes place on the island of Hawaii. The festival celebrates the rich history and cultural significance of Kona coffee, which is a type of coffee grown in the Kona region of Hawaii. The festival typically takes place in November and includes a variety of events, such as coffee tastings, culinary demonstrations, cultural workshops, and live music. It is a popular event among tourists and locals alike and is an opportunity to learn more about the history and culture of Kona coffee. The festival is also a time for people to come together and celebrate the unique food and drink culture of the islands. The Kona Coffee Cultural Festival is a great way for visitors to experience the rich culinary traditions of Hawaii and to support local coffee farmers and producers.

Hawaii International Film Festival (November)

The Hawaii International Film Festival (HIFF) is an annual event that takes place on the island of Oahu in Hawaii. The festival showcases a variety of independent and international films, and is a premier film event in the Pacific Rim. The festival typically takes place in the fall and includes a variety of events, such as film screenings, panel discussions, and special events. It is a popular event among tourists and locals alike, and attracts people from all over the world. The HIFF is an opportunity for film enthusiasts to experience a wide range of films and to learn more about the art of filmmaking. It is also a time for filmmakers to showcase their work and for industry professionals to network and discuss the latest trends and developments in the film industry.

CHAPTER 14

Getting around Big Island

There are many ways to get around and explore the tourist destinations on the Big Island of Hawaii. The most common form of transportation is by car, but you can also rent a motorbike or bicycle, take a taxi, or use public transportation such as the Hele-On bus system.

Car: Renting a car is the most common form of transportation on the Big Island. There are several car rental companies located on the island, such as Alamo, Hertz, and Thrifty. With a car, you can explore the island at your own pace, and it's the best way to get to many of the more remote destinations.

Motorbike/Bicycle: Renting a motorbike or bicycle is another option for getting around the Big Island. This is a great way to explore the island's many trails and roads, and it's perfect for those who want to take in the sights and sounds of the island at a slower pace.

Taxi: Taxis are also available on the Big Island and can be a convenient way to get around. Taxis can be booked online or through your hotel or vacation rental.

Public Transportation: The Hele-On bus system is an affordable way to get around the Big Island. There are bus routes that cover much of the island, and they are a great way to get to tourist destinations like the Hawaii Volcanoes National Park and the beaches of the Kona Coast.

No matter which form of transportation you choose, there are many ways to get around and explore the tourist destinations on the Big Island of Hawaii.

Conclusion

The Big Island of Hawaii is a must-see destination for travelers looking for an unforgettable vacation. From the stunning natural beauty of its beaches and forests to the vibrant culture of its locals, the Big Island offers something for everyone. There are endless activities to keep visitors busy, from snorkeling in the crystal clear waters of the Pacific Ocean to exploring the hidden wonders of the Volcanoes National Park. The Big Island also boasts some of the best restaurants in the state, offering an array of unique cuisines and flavors.

No trip to the Big Island is complete without a visit to the beautiful beaches. Whether you're looking to relax and soak up the sun, or get in some surfing and swimming, there's a beach for everyone. From the black sand beaches of Kaimu to the white sands of Hapuna, visitors will never be bored with the amount of beaches to explore.

The culture of the Big Island is also worth exploring. From the traditional hula dancing to the music of the ʻukulele, the island's culture is alive and vibrant. There are numerous festivals throughout the year, from the Merrie Monarch Festival, to the annual

Hawaii Island Festival. There are also plenty of opportunities to learn about Hawaiian history and culture at a variety of museums and cultural centers.

The Big Island also offers a wide range of outdoor activities, from hiking in the lush rainforests to horseback riding on the beaches. Visitors can also enjoy mountain biking, kayaking, and snorkeling. For those looking for a more relaxing experience, there are plenty of spas and wellness centers to help you unwind.

Overall, the Big Island of Hawaii is an amazing destination for any type of traveler. With its stunning natural beauty, vibrant culture, and endless activities, the Big Island is the perfect place to get away, relax, and create memories that will last a lifetime.

Made in United States
Orlando, FL
08 March 2023